Rethinking Our War on Poverty

2020 Edition

A View from Below the Line

Dwight Clough

WeWillEndPoverty.com

Rethinking Our War on Poverty

2020 Edition

A View from Below the Line

*I don't march in lockstep
with Democrats.*

*I don't march in lockstep
with Republicans.*

I don't play by their rules.

*That might make you angry.
Sorry.*

Rethinking Our War on Poverty

A view from below the line

I need to start here.

I know what it means to live below the poverty line. This isn't some college term paper. I didn't lead a focus group, send out surveys, or interview a university professor.

I've lived it. I know what it's like:

- To be hungry—to stand in a grocery store aisle looking at a can of beans that costs 65 cents and want it so bad, but not be able to afford it.

- To be homeless—with a wife and a baby girl. Yes, I had a car, and we drove down the highway past all the exits, but none of those exits was ours.

- To go bankrupt—not because I wanted to, but because I had no choice.

- To get medical bills I couldn't pay.

- To work for an entire year and not make a dime.

- For my children to look up at me and ask, "Daddy, are we poor?"

- To hide the truth from family and friends because I was too ashamed to tell people how little money we really had.

- To face foreclosure.

- To fear because my car was on the side of the road. I didn't know what was wrong, and I had no money to get it fixed.

- To have the brains and the drive to make north of $100,000 a year and yet be struggling to make $12,000, and sometimes far less.

- To have the state department of revenue write me a letter saying, "Based on the income you're reporting, we don't know how you survived." Guess what? I'm not sure I know either.

- To drive by the Dairy Queen and tell my kids (again, for the 100th time), "No, we can't stop. I don't have the money to buy you an ice cream cone."

- To watch yet another business endeavor crash and burn, or die a slow agonizing death.

- To feel the anger when I see my 16-year-old daughter snubbed by her "friends" because she doesn't have enough money to be cool.

This book comes out of my four decades of living below the line. This is a view from below the line.

Before we jump in, two other points:

1. The early Christian leader James said this in his writings: "Has not God chosen the poor to be rich in faith…" So, yeah, my faith is inseparable from who I am, and you'll see it bleed through on these pages.

2. I'm going to say some things in this book that will probably make you angry. I hope that's okay. I'm not trying to be provocative. I'm just trying to be honest and tell you the truth.

Rethinking what's possible

We can win.

We really can. And when I say we can win this war on poverty, I do NOT mean that we can increase welfare spending until you can't distinguish between the poor and the middle class.

That's not victory. That's giving up.

No, we can win. We can empower Americans to move across the poverty line to the point where the percentage of people who require assistance from the government becomes microscopically small. And we can do it without being unkind and unfair. We can empower people to win their own battle against poverty.

This can take place.

But it won't take place simply because the government passes a new law or starts a new program.

That's because the government, by itself, cannot solve poverty. It doesn't have that ability.

But we can. You and I and 327 million other Americans acting in concert can win this war. If we all get moving in the same direction, poverty could be nothing more than a memory ten years from now.

It is doable.

But winning will require us to rethink our strategy. If we don't—if we keep fighting the same fight, playing by the same rules—I can assure you: *We will not win.*

We will lose.

We need the combined courage to look at what we're doing and admit: This isn't working. Yes, we've made strides, but we're no where near victory. Instead, we're dug in, we're fighting a World War I trench war in the 21st century. We're not thinking clearly. We've lost our focus.

In a way, we've given up.

Over 20,000 days ago, President Lyndon Johnson declared his war on poverty. That's a long time to be at war.

The problem with a war that goes on for over 50 years is this: Pretty soon, it's all that people know. They don't know any different. They don't understand—we don't understand

—that war is abnormal. Wars are waged for one reason and one reason only—victory.

We need to win. We need to stop fighting and start winning.

I don't buy the notion that victory is impossible. If that's what you believe, then someone taught you to believe that, and you need to unlearn it.

Victory is possible, but, as this book will demonstrate, we need to re-imagine how that victory will take place.

Johnson's Great Society was a first step—noble maybe in its time—but now the Great Society has faltered. It cannot win this war. We need to embrace a new strategy, one that is liberal and conservative, radical and reactionary all at the same time. We need to get off the political spectrum and onto a solution that really works.

Rethinking our attitudes

To win the war on poverty, we need to change our mindset. Four attitudes need to go. These attitudes are ubiquitous, and they are wrong.

Indifference

The biggest reason we don't win is we don't care. It just doesn't matter to us. *If people are poor, it's their problem, it's not my problem, I don't care. Don't make me live next to them. Don't make me have a relationship with them. Keep them in their world and me in mine. Keep them out of sight so they can be out of mind. I don't care about them. I care about me.*

The cure for indifference, of course, is love. Or, if you don't like that word, then use the word value. We need to learn to value other people. That is the crowning virtue, and since we live in a culture that places low value on teaching virtues, it takes many people a lifetime to learn the virtue of love if they ever learn it at all.

If we want to win the war on poverty, we need to learn to value other people, starting with the person right in front of us. When we learn to care, everyone is enriched.

This requires a cultural revolution—certainly not in the Communist Chinese sense of the term—but a change in our values that cannot be created by the government. This must come from a grassroots transformation of our culture.

We need to learn to care.

Arrogance

I speak here of the arrogance of know-it-all elitists, smarter-than-thou social engineers, academic types, people who think they have all the answers, people who want to solve the problem of poverty without listening to the poor.

This arrogance is found in those who have a one-size-fits-all solution for poverty. It's found in those who herd people like cattle into categories and brand them with expected limitations. These are those who secretly think the poor are poor because they are stupid. (But they would never voice that opinion aloud for you to hear.) It is found in those who want to keep the poor on the plantation instead of truly setting them free. It is pernicious because it is disguised as social justice. The arrogant wear the mask of "caring for the poor." In so doing, they block every initiative that could truly help the poor.

The cure for arrogance, of course, is humility. The humility to listen, to learn—and unlearn, to truly understand. The arrogant have stopped learning because they think they're too smart to learn from anyone. Their growth has been stunted by their own pride. They need to listen. They need to understand. They need to break free from the shackles of their own narrative and view the world through a different set of eyes.

Contempt

By contempt, I mean the attitude that says, "I made my own way, why can't they?" I mean the belief shared by tens of millions of Americans that the poor are poor because they are lazy.

I don't know how many times I've heard, "Welfare recipients need to get off their lazy a---- and get a job."

Yeah. About that. The poor I know mostly have jobs. Some of them have two jobs, three jobs, four jobs.

This contempt can be particularly strong among those who make more money when they work harder. It's difficult for them to understand that others make <u>less</u> money when they work harder. Because of this, they assume that laziness accounts for poverty. But let me ask you: Would you work twice as hard for half as much money? Would you, really?

Let me explain it in a way that most people in the middle class can understand. Suppose you get laid off—no fault of your own, you lose your job.[1] While looking for a new job, you collect unemployment compensation. While you're out looking, you come across a nice part-time job. You would enjoy the work, and the extra money would come in handy. But you <u>don't</u> take it because you know the minute you do, you'll lose your unemployment benefits, and you need those benefits to pay your mortgage, buy groceries, and put gas in the car. You don't take it because you're smart enough to realize that taking it would shoot yourself in the foot.

---

1   As I work here on this 2020 Edition, we are in the midst of the COVID-19 lock down. Many good, hard-working middle class people <u>have</u> lost their jobs. If that's you, my heart goes out to you. I pray you will weather this storm and emerge stronger than ever.

For most of my journey through poverty, I've been self-employed. At times I've taken on jobs—driving, janitorial, whatever. But there were other times when I could have found work at a retail store or a fast food joint, but I chose not to take those jobs—to instead devote my energies to working on another business venture. Why? Because I knew that the job would consume a great deal of time and energy and take me nowhere. I would spend all this time working at some job, and, yes, at the end of the year my adjusted gross income would be higher. In exchange for a number that looks better on my taxes, my family would lose our health care coverage, earned income credit, Pell Grants, food share, whatever. We would be poorer. If I'm going to put energy into something, I'd rather put it into something that at least has the potential of carrying my family beyond the point of needing those things.

Some preach self reliance, but offer no prescription for moving from dependence to self reliance, other than to throw people off the dock into deep water and see who sinks and who swims. This Darwinian approach doesn't work. Sure, it works for some, but contempt leaves the rest in the deep water to drown.

Contempt does not solve poverty. Blame does not solve poverty. Respect does. And the poor have not been given the respect they deserve. Not by a wide, wide margin. When we start respecting people, we start listening to them, honoring them, seeing things through their eyes, working with them to find solutions that work in their world.

Political ambition

We need people with political influence. They can be powerful allies in this war against poverty. But too many of them are far more concerned about getting votes, than they are about solving poverty.

On one side, you have the party who claims to care about the poor, but, I suspect, cares far more about getting votes from the poor than it does actually care about the poor. If they cared about the poor they would work to get people out of poverty instead of keeping them dependent on their handouts.

On the other side, you have the party who has written off the poor. Most of the poor won't vote for them, so they will focus their attention on helping the people who will vote for them. In other words, they ignore the poor.

One party builds a zoo and places the poor in cages, promising to feed them. The other says, "Take away their food, and they'll find a way to break out of those cages."

In other words, neither party is interested in solving poverty. It's not in their inherent political interests to do so.

Political ambition comes first. Helping the poor comes last. Please understand what I'm saying. I'm _not_ saying that all politicians are evil people. Many are not. Many have good hearts. But the _system_ itself does little to motivate politicians to do the right thing. If politicians need to choose between getting votes and helping the poor, getting votes can be a powerful temptation.

The cure for political ambition is trust. People with political power need to earn the trust of the people who voted them into office. If they are hired or appointed, they need to earn the trust of the people they arc supposed to be serving.

I have a message for you who hold the office you hold because people voted for you.

We voted for you because we trusted you. Please don't violate that trust. Stop thinking along party lines, and start thinking about how to serve the people who count on you to act in their best interests. And I don't just mean the people who voted for you. I mean all of the people.

I believe ...

You are here for a reason.
You are designed to make a difference.
You are meant to bring eternal good into many many lives.

I can point to any person
and say those words
and those words are true.

I believe …
There's room in life for everyone to win.
I define winning as becoming what you were designed to be.

I cannot win in life
by making you lose.

We're all in this together.
When you win
I win.

When you hurt
I hurt.

Your success does not diminish me;
rather it enriches me.

I cannot truly become richer
by making you poorer.

I believe …
Money does not define your worth,
but when your potential is properly cultivated
and deployed,
and when the world works as it should,
money will follow.

I believe that helping one another
is not a sign of weakness;
it's a sign of wisdom.

If I can help you win
that's a win for all of us.

When we start believing these things
we can start seeing the poor through a different set of eyes.

We start seeing the vast
untapped
human treasure
that exists among low income people.

We start asking the question:
What can we do to release this treasure
for the benefit of us all?

Rethinking victory

The war on poverty isn't over until we win. And I don't think we've been very clear about what winning means. You can't win a war until you understand what it means to win.

Let me help. Here's what the world will look like when we win the war on poverty:

Freedom from failure

Failure is a great thing. It's a wonderful learning experience. Everybody ought to fail, at least once. If you've never failed, have you really lived? Have you taken a risk and tried to see what's possible?

But a lifetime of failure is not a good thing. A lifetime of living below your potential is not what life intends. For anyone.

There's a reason why you are here. You have value to offer to all the rest of us. And that value is worth enough so that you should not need to live in poverty. But finding that value and cultivating that value can be a tricky thing, and sometimes we need to help one another learn how to do that.

I don't mean the world owes you a living. It does not. I mean you have something of great value to offer. It's up to you to discover and deploy that value. It's up to all of us to help one another to do that.

We're all in this together. We're a team. We're on the same side. Like Jim Rohn once said, "There's just one problem with trying to sink half the boat—guess what happens to your half." Each person's success is a piece of the victory for all of us. Each person's failure is an opportunity for all of us—an opportunity to learn, to regroup, to find another way, to find an alternative path to victory.

Poverty ends when the value each person has to offer is discovered, embraced, recognized, and put to its best use.

Freedom from slavery

Obviously victory means an end to human trafficking and sex trafficking. But there are other types of slavery that need to end for us to plant the flag of victory:

1. Freedom from overwork

No one should need to work more than 50 hours per week *unless they want to*. Everybody needs a life. Everybody needs time with family, friends, faith, recreation. It's part of being human. Read the Ten Commandments; a reasonable workload means a day or two off each week. Victory over poverty means every family has the resources to take some kind of family vacation once a year.[2]

2. Freedom from misalignment

On top of this, nobody should spend a lifetime working a job they hate. Sure, for a season all of us need to work jobs we don't really like or work with people that aren't fun to be around. I've needed to do that and so have you. But nobody should be sentenced to that for an entire life. There needs to be a route out. If there isn't, you're still in poverty—I don't care how much money you make. Out there somewhere there's a good fit for each person that corresponds with that person's personality, passions, and abilities.

I want to pause here and underscore this. One size does not fit all. Each person is unique. Different from all others. Each person

---

2   Some of you of a conservative bent may be ready to throw this book against the wall because you think I'm advocating that the government pay for all of these things. Keep reading.

has a unique contribution to make. And the path out of poverty needs to be customized to that individuality.

If we fail to do this, if we try to herd the poor out of poverty like so many cattle, we will fail. Unique people require unique solutions. You can't win this war without getting to know the people you're trying to save.

3. Freedom from dependence

Yes, dependence enslaves. If I depend on someone to educate me, put food on my table, pay my doctor bills, then that "someone" becomes my master. The master (politicians, bureaucrats, whatever) controls me. The master can and will determine the content of my education, the type and quality of health care I receive, even the food I eat. The master holds the whip and the chains; the master barks the orders and, in order to receive those benefits, I must obey. The master can punish me at any time by taking away these benefits I thought were mine. The master controls. (And here we have one of the key reasons why we don't win the war on poverty. The master loves control. The master loves to press his boot on the necks of the poor.)

How do I get free from the master?

Self reliance.

Winning the war on poverty means moving from dependence to self reliance. Within the scope of reason, we all need to find a way to pay our own way.

How do we do that? I'm not seeing much in the way of clear thinking on this issue.

For example, many people mistakenly believe that ending poverty is only about providing opportunity, and they define opportunity as jobs.

I think that's naive.

Self reliance doesn't depend on opportunity alone. It also takes motivation and ability.

Motivation. You gotta want the opportunity. If you don't want it, you're not gonna take it. Simple, huh?

I guess not.

One day a woman in the neighborhood where I then lived asked to borrow my car. During the course of our conversation, it came out that she was on disability, apparently for some sort of mental illness. Then she said to me, "I'll do whatever it takes to keep that disability [payment]. If I have to climb up on the table for the doctor and crow like a rooster, I'll do it."

Was she legitimately disabled? I doubt it. You probably doubt it too.

You might cry, "Welfare fraud!" And, yes, you might be right.

You might have contempt for this woman, but I ask you this: Will your contempt get her out of poverty? Or, if that means nothing to you, then let me ask it this way: Will your contempt lower your taxes?

In my mind, this woman had just given me valuable information that the right person could use to get her out of poverty, and, as a consequence, potentially lower the taxes of the middle class. Here's what she told me: She has a survival strategy. That survival strategy is disability payments. She knows what she needs to do to get those payments, and she does it.

So what do we need to do to reorganize her thoughts? What do we need to do to inspire her to aim higher, to aspire for something greater? What happened to her to cause her to aim so low? How do we reverse that? What can we do to remove the internal barriers that prevent her from achieving her potential as a human being?[3]

---

3   Here I would like to recommend any of the books by Dr. Ruby K. Payne including *A Framework for Understanding Poverty* and *Bridges Out of Poverty*. Dr. Payne's insights are amazing, and her work has inspired thousands to make their way out of poverty.

I've never met a welfare caseworker who thinks in those terms. Almost every welfare caseworker I've ever met has this mindset: *We have a process for determining whether you're eligible for benefits or whether you are committing welfare fraud. Let me take you through that process.*

How does that get people out of poverty?

Hint: It doesn't.

Ability. Of course, opportunity means nothing without ability. If you don't have the ability, you can't take the opportunity.

I'm told that Bernie Sanders wants everyone to have free access to a college education. Most people who object to that say it will be too expensive.[4] And they might be right.

But let me ask you this: How are we going to get people qualified for the kinds of opportunities that take people out of poverty if we

---

4   I object to it for an entirely different reason. What the government funds, the government wants to micromanage because government is so intoxicated by controlling people and things. Good educational opportunities—apprenticeships, faith-based colleges, and others—would no doubt be excluded for a variety of mixed up political reasons. Curriculum would be prescribed by the Politburo of the United States. Just thinking about it almost makes me gag.

don't find a way to get them the education or training they need?

Somewhere along the line you gotta make strategic investments that will pay off in the end. Let's find a plan that works. I'm not necessarily saying that the government should pay for our education. Personally, I don't like it when the government pays for things—for the whole plantation reason cited above. But there's gotta be a way that people who need training can get the training they need. And I'm guessing that 327 million Americans can come up with a way.

If we want to.

Opportunity. Let's talk about opportunity.

Opportunities come in at least three flavors:

(1) Jobs. We need to figure out how to get the right jobs to the right people. Getting people trained for the right jobs is a big part of that. We need to create paths of upward mobility that move good people out of dead end jobs into growth jobs.

(2) Self employment or business. Some people are wired to be entrepreneurs, shopkeepers, solopreneurs, artists, church planters,

and the like. They just need the right coaching, the right team to get them established.

(3) Marriage or family. Don't laugh, and don't write this one off. We bring value to our world in many different ways. A strong and healthy marriage can create an income producing team where each partner can have a different but equally important role. And, no, I'm not trying to take us back to the 1950s, I'm just saying, let's think outside the box.

Within certain limitations, ability can be taught, motivation can be coached, and opportunity can be created. But all of this takes us working together as a team.

Levels of reliance.

I don't think we should look at self reliance as an all-or-nothing kind of thing. Instead, there are levels of reliance.

#1 Self[5]—In an ideal world, each family should have at least one able-bodied adult of sound mind who is economically self-reliant.

---

5   Maybe Les Stroud can survive all on his own, but the rest of us need one another. Together we create an infrastructure that allows the individual to flourish. In that sense, none of us is self reliant; we all live with some level of interdependence, interconnection, and trust.

That isn't always possible, but we can aim for that.

#2 Family—If self reliance isn't possible, family should be the first line of defense. In a good family, accountability, trust, respect, understanding, and love should be high. No family is perfect, but a good family provides much better care than the next three alternatives. As a culture let's work on creating good families.

#3 Circle of care—I'm imagining here church congregations, friends, coworkers, and similar groups. When help is needed outside the family, the closest non-family circle of care could and should step up to the plate. I admit, we have a long, long way to go before this will be a reality for most people who need it, but I think it's something we should aim for. As a culture, most of us are not very good at putting ourselves in someone else's shoes, and we have very little patience with those whose life experience is different than our own. A pity. If we could raise our level of understanding, respect, and trust, we could enrich our lives by caring for one another.

#4 Community—The community understands its own needs. When the circle of care cannot be there, can the community can step in to fill the gap?[6]

#5 State—Finally we come to the state, that is, the government—the least desirable, but most often employed. Why is it the least desirable? Here's the reality: The state doesn't care about you. At all. If you cease to exist, the state is unmoved. The state doesn't know you; the state doesn't want to know you—at least not for any benevolent purposes. Getting people out of poverty requires a great deal of respect, patience, understanding, care, and love. The state is totally impotent in those areas.

What we have here is the ladder of self reliance. The bottom rung is dependence on the state. The second rung is empowerment from the community. The third rung is support from the circle of care. The fourth rung is care from the family. And the final rung is self reliance.

Helping people move up this ladder is a key to winning the war on poverty.

---

6   See *Bridges to Sustainable Communities: A systemwide, cradle-to-grave approach to ending poverty in America* by Philip E. DeVol.

The right kind of debt can open doors. But the wrong kind of debt enslaves. The poor know the wrong kind of debt only too well.

What do you do when you're in so much pain you can't think straight? You take the credit card, you go to the dentist or the chiropractor or that person not covered by Medicaid, and you rack up a debt you can't pay. There's nothing in the house but an almost empty box of saltines. You're hungry, but because of some glitch you're not eligible for food stamps. The kids need diapers, but food stamps doesn't cover it. Rent is due, but you spent the little money you had fixing the car. Again.

Survival debt. Anybody who has lived below the poverty line knows what I'm talking about.

I'm not saying every person should be debt free, but every one should be able to see their way out of debt within a reasonable length of time.

Freedom from fear

Here's what I mean:

1. Safety

No one—no matter what race, religion, gender, or any other category—should live in fear of attack, abuse, theft, or intimidation. No one should be afraid in their own home. No one should be afraid to step out of their home. No one should be afraid to walk through their own neighborhood or any other neighborhood.

Victory means safety.

2. Freedom from worry

Victory in the war on poverty means that no one should worry about food, clothing, health care, safe and reliable transportation, affordable and comfortable housing, and other necessities.

Here I need to pause and talk about health care.

I'm not a huge fan of Obamacare, but it's a whole lot better than nothing. I didn't like the mandate—that was wrong. I don't like the very confusing tax issues. I don't like spending 50 hours (no lie) with the Health Insurance Marketplace just to change my address.

I hate bureaucracies.

Before he was elected, Trump said repeal and replace. I don't know if he had an idea in mind, or if he was hoping that his jealous-of-Trump Republican comrades would come up with an idea, but, of course, it hasn't happened (as of this writing), and now with a divided Congress, it probably won't happen.

Why? Because making Trump look bad is far more important to many politicians than helping him do something good for the people of America.

But I digress.

Do I like the government taking over health care? No, I do not. Do I like socialized medicine? No, I don't. But, if it comes down to a choice between my sick child dying and socialized health care, I'll take socialized health care every time. Here's what I'm saying: You can't just give me solutions that work for the middle class unless and until you figure out a way to get everyone out of poverty.

So, yes, repeal and replace. Go for it. In the process, see if you can get rid of the systemic incompetence of the current system. A website that doesn't work. When your income goes below the threshold, they kick you off without explanation. (Come on, people! This is the 21st century. You have the technology to move someone from Obamacare to Medicaid without making that person spend 10 hours on the phone with some bureaucrat, and send the same documents over and over again to some office where some lazy government worker doesn't bother to read them.)

Okay, that was a rant. Sorry.

We need to do a couple things with health care.

First, we need to get rid of the canyon. For the poor, making more money can be very scary because the first thing we ask is this: *What will happen to my health care?* Will I lose health insurance? Or, between premium payments, spotty coverage, deductibles, and co-payments, will my health care be way too expensive for me? This creates a huge canyon that the poor must leap across in order to move from poverty to middle class. It creates a barrier that keeps poor people poor.

Second, we need to figure out how to decrease medical costs. I've heard a variety of suggestions including: stop overcompensating doctors; get people into preventative care; get rid of the AMA. I don't know if those are good ideas or bad ideas. I just know that we need to think about this. Would it work for the government pay for medical school and pay for malpractice insurance, then for doctors agree to adjust their fees for the patient's income? Or, what if the government takes care of catastrophic insurance for everyone so that no one goes bankrupt, and then health insurance companies create plans appropriate for different income levels?

I don't know. I'm thinking aloud. You probably have better ideas than I do, and that's great. Let's get those good ideas out there, and then fund what works.

Freedom from fractured families

Every child needs a dad.

I know some people are going to howl when they read that. But I stand by it. There's too much evidence that suggests that children from stable, two-parent homes are in a better place than children who don't have that benefit.

Are there exceptions? Of course. You may be one of them.

Am I trying to lay a guilt trip on single parents? Of course not. You have it hard enough without taking any guff from me.

But I am saying this: As a culture, we need to teach young men to be fathers. And by that I do NOT mean how to impregnate a young woman and then move on to the next conquest. I mean staying. I mean going the distance. I mean being there. Being present. Being a rock of stability for your wife and children. Learning to be a leader in your home alongside your wife without being abusive or controlling. Learning to be someone your children look up to, admire, and want to emulate.

Government will not teach this. Public schools could teach it, but probably won't for a whole variety of social and political reasons. So it falls on the ailing church and the ailing family as institutions to pick up the slack. If we don't do it, who will?

We won't win our war on poverty until we find these fathers who are missing in action, and bring them home, mentoring them, and equipping them to be the men they were designed to be.

In the 1960s we jettisoned marriage, monogamy, and morality. Suggesting that we return to those "archaic" values is like wetting your pants in public. But, if you ask me, free love isn't free. It seems to take most people most of their lives to figure that out, and some people never get it.

Women are not disposable sex objects. And, by the way, men are not disposable either.

Government cannot and will not teach this, but the state certainly could cooperate a little bit.

When our daughter was born with birth defects, and we had no insurance to pay for the surgery she needed, someone told me to sign up for Medicaid. So I went in and filled out an application. The caseworker took my application, ripped it up before my eyes, and filled another one out with my wife's name as the applicant.

Hmm.

What message do you pick up from that?

Rethinking our narratives

Some time ago, my wife was shopping at a thrift store. When she arrived at the register to pay for her purchases, she saw that the person in front of her had stepped away from the cashier. My wife, thinking the other woman had completed her purchases, began engaging the cashier. Belatedly, my wife realized that the other woman's transaction was not yet complete, and my wife had interrupted.

"I am so sorry," my wife said to the other shopper who happened to be African American.

"It's okay," she replied, "It's a white world."

What just happened? I surmise the following: In the mind of the other shopper, she is a member of an oppressed minority. My wife is a member of the dominant class. Here's yet another example of the dominant class throwing their weight around. In my wife's mind, the incident had nothing to do with race, but instead was an example of unintentional rudeness brought about by a misinterpretation of the other shopper's actions.

Exact same event—vastly different interpretations.

I'm not trying to argue that one interpretation was true or justified and one was not. I'm merely trying to point out that we each have stories that we tell ourselves that allow us to interpret life and life's events. I call these stories narratives.

And our narratives are the lenses through which we see our world. As a result, none of us is objective. Only God is objective. The rest of us see our world through the filter of our own narrative. And that narrative bends reality until it's shaped the way we think it should be shaped.

Most people, I think, don't realize how important these narratives are. Because we each tell ourselves a different story, we live in vastly different realities even though we occupy the same planet and experience the same events.

It's easy to assume that others are telling themselves the same story we are, but, in fact, they are not. And because they are not, their opinions and behaviors often mystify us entirely.

The sales job

People of influence try to sell their narrative to you. Parents, for example, try to sell their narrative to their children—with mixed results.

Educators are selling you a narrative. They want you to interpret your world according to the story they tell. They claim to be wise, knowledgeable, studied, intelligent, and correct. These claims—valid or not—are well marketed, and they reinforce the educator's sales pitch.

Journalists are selling you a narrative. They want you to swallow their story; they want you to believe their explanation for what the world looks like and why. I know they pretend to be objective, factual, and authoritative. But that's all part of the sales presentation. Those are tools they use to convince you their narrative is the one you should adopt. I'm not saying their narrative is necessarily wrong. It might be right on the money. Then again, it might be a million miles away from the truth.

Politicians, entertainers, advertisers, religious leaders—they're all selling you a narrative. I'm selling you a narrative. That's the purpose of this book. That's the purpose of every book.

In an ideal world, people of influence would be wiser than the rest of us. We could then adopt their narratives—start telling ourselves their stories—without further thought or examination.

But that is not reality. People of influence are pushier than other people. They're better sales people. They're better connected. But they're not necessarily wiser.

Here's another consideration: For our own mental health, our narratives must remain stable. We can't daily change the story we tell ourselves because this would lead to internal chaos. For example, if I changed my narrative a certain way, one day I would believe that my wife loves me, the next day I would believe she hates me. Her actions would not change, but my narrative changes, and, with it, my reality changes.

All of this creates two different kinds of tension:

(1) The struggle for dominance. People of influence are trying to get us to change our narrative, and we naturally resist doing that.

However, the only way we truly grow as individuals and as a culture is to change our narrative, swapping a bad story for a good story, hopefully swapping lies for truth. In fact, true transformation comes when we change our narrative at a primal level. These paradigm shifts turn us into better people, and, collectively, into a better society.

Let me give you an example. For many years whenever my wife got sick, I got angry. Why would I do that? It all had to do with a story I was telling myself—one that I wasn't even aware I was believing. When I was growing up, I told myself the story that when my mom got sick, there was no one to protect me.

This became ingrained as part of my narrative: *When the woman in your life is sick, you are not safe.* This was below the level of my conscious awareness, but it was there nevertheless.

Anyway, I was processing all of this with God one day, and He changed my narrative. The woman in my life could be sick, and I could still be okay.

Hmm. Interesting. Next time my wife got sick, I didn't get angry. I was okay. She was sick. I was her husband. I could help her.

I underwent a paradigm shift that changed the story I tell myself. As a result, I'm a better person. I grew as a person.

All of us need to do this. We need to grow. We need to find those better stories and adopt them.

(2) There is also a tension between the stories we tell ourselves and the facts. When facts don't fit our narrative, we usually throw away the facts and keep the narrative.

This is why we will ignore the faults of a candidate from the political party of our preference, and ignore the strengths of a candidate from a political party that doesn't support our narrative.

As a person of faith, I am troubled, for example, by the narrative held by some in the media that Christianity is the religion of white colonialists who use it as a weapon to dominate and oppress.

Part of the reason this troubles me is that millions of Christians have been slaughtered for their faith. In over 50 nations worldwide, it is dangerous or illegal to be a Christian. Believers are routinely harassed, fined, arrested, imprisoned, tortured, and even executed for their faith. All of this is well documented. But it almost never gets covered by the media. Why? The facts don't fit their narrative.

Money and poverty

What does all of this have to do with poverty? Simple. A big reason why we don't win the war on poverty is that we hold narratives that get in the way.

For example, many people tell themselves that poor people are lazy. Maybe some of them are, but that has not been my experience or observation. Instead, the poor people I know are some of the hardest working people I've ever met. Some people hold the narrative that poor people are stupid sheep who need to be herded and watched over by the intellectual elite. (Of course, they would never use those words, but read between the lines.)

I think these narratives are neither helpful nor accurate. Laziness and stupidity are not confined to or concentrated within any economic class. There's plenty to go around. Nor are they, in my view, the primary causes of poverty.

Some hold the view that poor people are morally deficient. Maybe some are, just as some in the other economic classes are. But I don't think moral deficiency explains poverty.

Narratives are not always right or wrong. Sometimes, they're just different. For example, people think differently about money. Examples:

The Middle Class Approach. The middle class looks at money like this: Get a good education, then get a good job. Get a comfortable home in the suburbs. Drive a nice car. The harder you work, the more money you make. Poverty is for lazy people. Don't take risks. Whatever you do, don't lose your job. You need your job. Avoid debt. Get good benefits (health insurance, etc.), and a good retirement package. Be a good employee. Work your way up the corporate ladder. This is success.

The Investor Approach. The investor looks at money like this: Keep your living expenses as low as possible. Make more money than you need. Put the excess into investments. Keep that money growing. Manage risk. Get the benefits of business without the headaches. Shelter your investments from taxes if you can. Stay frugal and invest well, so your investments will eventually support you.

Retire in your 40s or 50s, enjoy life, maybe travel the globe.

The Business Approach. A business person looks at money like this: I'm getting paid to take a risk, but I don't take stupid risks. I've studied the market. I know what people want to buy. I know where to get it or how to make it, and I can deliver it. Furthermore, I can create jobs for people who will help me give customers what they want. The business person is willing to work much harder than the average employee. You gotta get an incredible number of things right to really make it big in business. And that requires a unique combination of skill and incredible circumstances.

The Artist Approach. The artist (author, actor, painter, comedian, whatever) thinks of money like this: I have something inside that I must express. I can't do otherwise. I sure hope I get paid for it. Artists hope to ride the wave of popularity and/or create something that brings in ongoing royalties. One percent make it big. J.K. Rowling became a billionaire. The other 99% eat macaroni and cheese. But some artists (not many) improve their chances by thinking like business people.

The Faith Approach. The person who lives by faith looks at money like this: I take my marching orders from God. All money belongs to Him. I belong to Him. He will provide what I need when I need it. I'm going to be faithful and work hard at whatever task He gives me, even if I don't like it, and He will provide what I need. Risk, impossibility, adventure are everyday realities that the person who lives by faith learns to enjoy. If you're called to live by faith, be prepared to have your own faith tested—and that of everyone around you.

I don't necessarily think that one of those approaches is better than another, I think they're just different. But we can't even start talking about winning the war against poverty until we acknowledge that different narratives exist—they aren't necessarily right and wrong; they're just different.

We need to hear one another's stories. We need to ponder them. We need to understand them. We need to respect one another—even when we tell ourselves different stories, even when we disagree.

Human value

Here's another way in which we need to rethink our narratives: How do we measure someone's worth?

Often, we measure value in dollars. But that doesn't always work. People bring value in ways that cannot be measured by dollars.

Take Mother Teresa, for example. To the best of my knowledge, she did not engage in commerce. She didn't make a profit for some corporation. Technically speaking, she didn't hold down a job. All her money was given to her. She received donations from other people who worked. Yet she brought great value into our world, and I don't think most people are going to dispute that.

Children. Almost without exception they cannot earn their own way in life. Yet, when those children are our own, we put great value on them. If we don't, there's something seriously wrong.

People with disabilities. Although I think we can train almost anyone to do some kind of job, business, or craft, there are exceptions. Some people cannot work. While I don't have personal experience with folks who have severe disabilities, the people I've talked to who do tell me that caring for these folks has brought a dimension of value into their lives they never imagined could be there.

Homemakers. In some families, one partner elects to stay home and create a warm, nurturing, caring environment for the family. Often, but not always, these are stay-at-home moms who want to give their small children the security and love that a day care facility simply cannot provide. I feel our culture has undervalued homemakers. In my view, it's a mistake to measure a person's worth by how much money s/he makes.

Rethinking political parties

Here in the US, two political parties hold 95% of the political power.

This, in my opinion, is a problem.

Who cares?

One party claims to care about the poor. Many, many people believe they really do care about the poor.

I don't.

If they really cared about the poor, they would get the poor out of poverty. If they really cared about the poor, welfare caseworkers would not spend 99% of their time trying to prevent welfare fraud and 0% of their time actually trying to help people get out of poverty.

Why doesn't the political party that pretends to care about the poor get people out of poverty? The answer is simple. If they get the poor out of poverty, then they no longer have a reason to exist. They can't campaign on "I care about the poor" any more because there won't be any poor. The group that votes them into office will be gone. They lose power. So it is not in their political best interests to get the poor out of poverty no matter how much they claim to care about the poor.

Again, I'm not saying that individual politicians don't care about the poor. Maybe they do. I'm saying the *political system* gives these politicians no real reason to care about the poor. And I'm certainly not saying that those who vote for these politicians don't care about the poor. I believe many do.

The other party ignores the poor. Poor people, as a group, don't vote for this party, so why should this party care about the poor? Why should this party pay any attention to the poor.

Once again, individual politicians in this party may care about the poor. Those who vote for this party may care about the poor. But the *political system* gives these political leaders no reason to care about the poor.

The bottom line is this: The political system encourages members of both parties to be way more committed to their own political power than they are to genuinely helping the poor.

One party needs people to be poor. And the other party needs to focus on people who aren't poor. In this way, the two-party system helps to cement poverty in place.

Stupid or lazy?

Another problem is perspective.

One political party thinks the poor are stupid. The other political party thinks the poor are lazy.

Thanks.

Neither is true, but both are widely believed.

Categories or individuals?

Another problem is what I call category politics vs. the power of the individual. One party places everyone in categories. It places me in categories. Because I am white, heterosexual, Protestant (worse still—Evangelical), and male I belong to the categories of the oppressors; therefore, I am an oppressor. I have white privilege. I have male dominance. And so on. Because I am an oppressor, I need to be suppressed.

Right. Sure. How can you say that about me if you don't even know me?

The other party says categories are meaningless; every individual has the power to transcend the limitations of his or her category.

Yeah. About that…

Some do, yes. Many don't. Why is that? If we're going to win the war on poverty, we need to find solutions for everyone, not just for the exceptional few.

This DOES NOT MEAN one-size-fits-all solutions—there are no such things. This does not mean government imposed limitations on those who achieve. This does not necessarily mean new legislation.

But it does mean we as a people, a society, a nation, a culture must find ways to help one another. With the right coaching and mentoring, maybe all of us can transcend the limitations that have been imposed on us. We must find ways to bridge our differences and come to the aid of one another.

Polarization

Meanwhile, I hate the polarization that turns friends into enemies. I hate politics—by that I mean I hate it that people scrap for power and influence and our world is often ruled by bullies who get to the top by pushing everyone else out of the way.

I hate it.

I have a "friend" who is a professor of economics at a major university. I put "friend" in quotes because he has so much contempt for me and for my opinions that I don't think you could call him a friend. But here he is—he's never been poor, never been homeless, never owned a business, never had to make a payroll —I've been in all of those positions—and he lectures me about poverty, minimum wage, capitalism, free enterprise—and tells me I don't have a right to an opinion because he is so much more educated than I am.

Here's what troubles me about that. Years ago, we were good friends. But now he despises me because I see things differently than he does. What kind of world do we live in where a difference of opinion fosters that kind of contempt?

On a Facebook thread I shared with him a thought that departed a baby step from the Intellectual Plantation, and I noticed that one of his friends immediately blocked me. Heaven forbid that we should listen to someone who doesn't march in lockstep with the Elite.

In case you're wondering what the thought was that was so offensive, here it is: I suggested that rather than raising the minimum wage to $20 an hour that we look for ways to get the people who are trying to support their families into better jobs and let people who were just entering the workforce—high school students—take these cheaper jobs. That way we wouldn't all need to pay $25 in 2010 dollars for a burger at McDonald's.

I mean what good does it do to hike the minimum wage if you can't buy anything with your newfound wealth because everything just became too expensive?

I didn't even mention that a major hike in the minimum wage also hurts starving artists, poor entrepreneurs, and anyone trying to escape poverty by starting a business. It helps big business and hurts small business. It increases the capital required to start a business, making business ownership even further out of reach for the poor.

My fantasy

The best thing that could happen to this country is a complete reboot. We need to scrap political parties and scrap the media, bring people together to listen to each other instead of yelling at each other, learn something from one another, and start fresh. I don't look for that to happen any time soon because people are so addicted to their precious little bit of power, but that's what we need.

In the absence of that, I look for leaders—people with the courage to buck the existing power structures and bring good people together around solutions that move our country forward. Expect these leaders to be vilified in the media, and "investigated" and, if possible, prosecuted by party politicians. (Remember, it was party politicians who crucified Jesus Christ.) But this kind of courageous leadership is what we need, and I dearly hope you are out there somewhere.

Rant over.

Rethinking class warfare

I've lived most of my life below the poverty line. Here's what goes through my mind when people tell me that they want to narrow the gap between the rich and the poor:

I don't care.

That's right. I don't care. If Jeff Bezos and Bill Gates suddenly become twice as rich as they are today, that's fine by me. More power to them. I'm cheering them on. If Warren Buffet's investments double overnight—that's fantastic as far as I'm concerned. Good for him. I have a son who wants to become another Warren Buffet, so if Warren Buffet does well, that's just more inspiration for my son.

I don't care how rich wealthy people are. I care about getting people like myself out of poverty. That's what I care about.

As a poor person, I'm insulted by the idea that we need to punish the rich. It conjures up the image of everyone going to a single pot of money, and the rich take out the lion's share of the money, leaving the poor with the scrapings. I'm not stupid enough to think that's how the real world works.

Okay, okay. I probably need to say this: Sure, some rich people are complete jerks. Some poor people are complete jerks. And some middle class people are complete jerks. But it's not my job to figure out who doesn't deserve the money they have, and it certainly isn't the job of some social justice warrior who fails to pause to get their facts straight before they rush to judgment on someone they don't understand.

As a rule, the rich became rich by creating jobs for the poor and the middle class. As a rule, they don't steal wealth from the poor. Instead, they create wealth. And why is creating wealth somehow criminal?

As long as there are rich people, and as long as there's some kind of economic mobility in this country, the richer they are, the more it gives us poor people something to shoot for. Why take away our dreams by punishing those who succeed?

Having said that, I do believe the rich have an important responsibility in the war on poverty. More on that later. First, let me comment on capitalism.

Capitalism or socialism?

Am I saying that unbridled capitalism is always wholesome and good?

No. Those who are unable to see the evils of capitalism are just as blind as those who are unable to see the evils of socialism. Enormous evil has been committed in the name of either system.

But as a rule, I do prefer capitalism. Here's why: It provides many more exit ramps from poverty than socialism does. Capitalism favors the creation and rise of small business, and small business gives consumers choice, and consumer choice contributes to economic prosperity.

So, yes, I'm a free market guy as long as the free market behaves. When it doesn't, I'm not. When the cost of an EpiPen® goes from under $100 to over $600[7] just because some multi-national pharmaceutical company can get away with it, then hey, free market goes out the window for me.

---

7 Sheila Kaplan, "F.D.A. Approves Generic EpiPen That May Be Cheaper," *New York Times*, Aug. 16, 2018. https://www.nytimes.com/2018/08/16/health/epipen-generic-drug-prices.html

Socialism concentrates power into the hands of the state. That might not be so bad if the state was always run by benevolent people. But that is not the case. The state is often run by people who care about being in power. If they must make a choice between their own power and caring for the people they serve (i.e., all the rest of us), they will choose their own power almost every time. [8]

You might object, saying that socialism redistributes wealth to the poor. Nah. It moves people down on the scale of self reliance, and up on the scale of dependence. In so doing, it makes everyone poorer.

As for communism, here we have a system that is ideologically evil. It is founded upon murdering all the people who know how to make money, followed by torturing, suppressing, and murdering all people of faith. "Religion… is the opiate of the masses," said Karl Marx, the founder of communism. Communism isn't "good in theory" and bad in execution. It's bad in theory and worse in execution.

---

8   People say that power corrupts. I don't think so. Power just magnifies what's already there. And what is already there? In most people: evil. Sorry, that's just the way it is. Sure, there might be some good there too, but the evil will be magnified.

Communists talk of "liberation," but they have never liberated a single soul. Communist countries are inevitably run by thugs. Stalin said, "The death of one man is a tragedy, the death of millions is a statistic." Those are not empty words. Stalin and sociopath communist leaders like him have murdered at least 65 million innocent people, and the real number is probably much higher. Communism robs people of hope and fills the life of the average person with misery, while a tiny group of party members live in absolute luxury. It is a sham, and I struggle to imagine anything that could be worse for overcoming poverty.

Tax the rich?

I agree that rich people should take the lead in helping poor people get out of poverty. But not in the way that is normally proposed: *taxing the rich*. When I say "taxing the rich," I mean imposing a punitive tax on the rich that is a far higher percentage than that paid by the middle class.

That isn't smart for several reasons:

1. The money goes into the wrong hands. Taxing the rich just puts more money in the hands of the same bureaucrats and politicians

who have failed win the war on poverty for 55 years. This will not help the poor.

2. Taxing the rich takes jobs away from the poor and the middle class. Politicians know this. That's why they create loopholes for the rich, and they will never close them, no matter what they say. They're lying to you because they know that those lies will get you to vote for them.

3. Why are we focused on making the rich poorer? Shouldn't we be focused on making the poor richer?

4. Class warfare has been tried, and it has failed. The Soviets are a prime example. They got rid of their rich, and then everybody was poor. People had to wait in line for 8 hours for a head of cabbage and another 5 hours for a potato. Great system.

5. Taxing the rich just discourages the poor. As someone who has lived most of my life below the poverty line, it just makes me think: No! Don't cut off my escape route from poverty. Let me at least have something to hope for, to aim for, to try to achieve. The longer I'm poor, the richer I need to get just to catch up with where I would have been if I were middle class.

6. It won't work. Even if you took all the money away from the rich and gave it to the poor, in five years the poor would be poor again, and the rich would be rich again. This is not because the poor deserve to be poor and the rich deserve to be rich, but rather because the rich have certain skills that the poor don't have, but the poor badly need.

My own war on poverty

Most likely to succeed

If my high school had voted on a "most likely to succeed," I would have been a strong contender. I was a high achiever. I got nearly straight A's with very little effort. While I didn't do sports, I did quite well in competitive debate and forensics (public speaking). As a sophomore I helped our team win several tournaments, and, along the way, accumulated a case full of trophies. We were one of the best teams in the state, and we even won a couple rounds in a national tournament.

Because my Christian faith was important to me, I turned down a partial scholarship to Cornell University and enrolled instead in Chicago's Moody Bible Institute. Back then Moody offered a three-year diploma instead of a four-year degree. After I graduated with that diploma, I was confronted with the three realities.

1. I found my bride at Moody. Since we got married a few months after I graduated, I

needed to find a job. More college didn't seem workable for me at the time.

2. I needed to put the idea of getting a full-time Christian ministry job on hold. My experience at Moody left me confused and conflicted about my faith. I'm not blaming that on Moody; I'm just saying I had things to sort out before I moved forward with ministry. I did eventually sort things out, but that took decades.

3. My three-year diploma was nearly useless out in the secular work world. It was barely better than a high school diploma.

I had originally intended to to pursue further education. I always assumed I would get a PhD in something. Problem was, I needed to make money now, and I didn't have a clear idea of where I wanted to go with further education. So I never obtained that additional schooling.

In retrospect, that was probably a mistake.

Instead, I got a job as a parole and probation officer for the State of Ohio. They liked me, and they waived their normal requirement for a four-year degree and accepted my three-year diploma. Nice.

But after four years as a parole officer, I realized I wasn't getting where I wanted to go. The job paid the rent and put gas in my car, but it did little more. I needed something that would take me to the next level.

Big bucks

I thought I found that something when I joined a multi-level marketing company. Promises of big bucks motivated me to quit my job, move to Madison, Wisconsin, and try my hand at self employment.

I was terrible.

I was a rotten salesman. I had no idea how to prospect, how to to recruit, how to develop prospects into customers or "downline." Although I tried.

The people who were making it big advised me to go after successful people because success breeds success. Hmm. I set my sights on a real estate tycoon in our city. Like a miniature version of Donald Trump, he owned a building with his name on it. After several weeks of trying, I finally made it past his palace guard, and got a 15-minute meeting with him.

In my pocket was my secret weapon: a non-negotiable, laminated copy of a $25,000 check that someone in our organization had earned in one month! That was more money that I could imagine earning in a year, much less one month. Surely this would entice Mr. Tycoon into paying attention to me.

I parked my little red Chevette next to a fleet of black Cadillacs in the parking lot. I took the elevator to the top floor where his secretary took my overcoat, and I marched into his office wearing my gray, pin-striped, three-piece suit, praying that the heel of my right black polished boot wouldn't fall off as it had a tendency to do. I wasted no time. I handed him the laminated copy of the check.

As I did, it suddenly occurred to me that the $25,000 check had lost a lot of value on that trip up the elevator. His desk was probably worth more than $25,000.

"What's this?" he asked.

I stammered something about how you could earn this kind of money if you only joined our multi-level marketing team and sold soap along with all the rest of us.

"We wouldn't be interested," he said, handing the check back to me.

"But, but…" My mind searched frantically for something, anything I could say that would change his mind.

"We wouldn't be interested," he repeated with finality.

I turned to leave. His secretary was right there with my overcoat in her hands. Evidently, she knew it would be a short meeting.

Let me summarize that experience: I worked for a year and made zero dollars. In fact, I lost money. My wife kept us alive by cleaning houses.

The eight mile rule

Somewhere along the line, I started writing resumes for people. That provided a decent part-time income. Meanwhile, my wife's housecleaning business started to flourish. I joined her. We hired employees. Things were looking up.

Then we moved. This was before cell phones, back in the day when your phone number advertised your location, and people were super sensitive to a vendor's location.

People didn't want to drive eight miles to get their resume written, and they assumed we would charge way too much to clean their homes if we had to drive eight miles. Both our little enterprises nosedived, as we scrambled to find a way to pay higher expenses at our new place. We tried everything we could think of to salvage both businesses, but all went up in smoke.

Homeless

I handed the rent check to the landlord and told him this would be our last month there. Where would we go? No idea.

We ended up homeless with a little baby with birth defects from February 29, 1992 to October 1, 1992. I gotta tell you, that is weird —driving down the highway and realizing that none of these exits are yours. We stayed part of the time in a friend's basement, part of the time wherever we could. Yes, friends and family helped. And no, we never had to sleep in the streets. For that I'm grateful.

At the same time this was going on, I had fallen behind in both our personal and employee payroll taxes. That, of course, is a major no no with the IRS. So we were in trouble with them, and I was doing my best to figure out a way to make payments. We did eventually get that tax debt paid, but it took time and a lot of uncomfortable phone calls with government bureaucrats.

While we were homeless, I found a job driving a school bus for disabled children. And we cleaned houses when we could. We actually still had a couple employees when we were homeless, if you can believe that. Somehow, we got their wages paid even though we didn't have enough money to pay for an apartment for ourselves.

After about seven months, we scraped together enough money to get a small apartment. A few months later, I got a better job first driving a transit bus, then shuttling corporate executives from Madison, Wisconsin to Chicago every day. We were once again approaching the bottom end of middle class. But then the day our third child was born, my job ended. Nobody's fault; these things just happen.

So I got unemployment—for one month, then nothing.

9/11

In the middle of figuring out how to support of a family of five with zero money, I bumped into a friend from high school. He was making big bucks as an employment recruiter. So he invited me to do some contract work for him. I did that for a couple years and actually moved from poverty to lower middle class. I made enough money for us to purchase our first home.

Soon after we bought that home, the 9/11 attacks occurred. The manufacturing industry took a hit, and my contract with my friend ended.

Meanwhile, I had written a couple books. I thought maybe I could make it as a Christian author.

That didn't work. In two years our annual income went from $35,000 to $2,500. Yep, you got that right. Six person[9] family trying to survive on two thousand five hundred dollars per year income.

I ran up credit card debt trying to survive. As you might be able to imagine, you can only live so long on credit cards. Sooner or later

---

9   Our 4th and final child was born in 1998.

those credit card companies want to be repaid. And I had no money to repay them.

I didn't want to declare bankruptcy. I didn't plan things that way, or intend to. But there we were. I had no other choice. I studied the bankruptcy statutes and wrote my own case. I managed to scrape together enough money to get a bankruptcy attorney to look at what I wrote and tell me how to fix it.

Nickels and doughnuts for pay

Meanwhile, the bank threatened to foreclose on our home. That was unpleasant. We had four little children, and no real prospects for a different place to live.

Just when all seemed lost, I found an opportunity to travel to the Gulf Coast to do some contract work for FEMA soon after the 2004 and 2005 hurricanes. And, about this same time, a friend came up to me and asked if our family would like to take over cleaning a 40,000 square foot bowling alley. I said yes. So we got the kiddos out of bed at 4:30 in the morning and we went down to the bowling alley as a family and cleaned it.

The kids got nickels and doughnuts for pay. We got enough money to pay the mortgage and put gas in the car.

I'm skipping over various enterprises I tried which failed. A few examples:

The next great online business

Some people who claimed to represent a search engine that came before Google promised to set me up with a lucrative, scaleable employment website. I engaged a project manager and hired and trained a bunch of people. I worked on this for months. When it came time for the search engine guys to deliver, they disappeared.

I came up with the idea to create a social networking site for people who wanted to make their world a better place—people with dreams. We'd connect dreamers, doers, mentors—and make good things happen. I put together a team, and we worked on it, but it never went anywhere.

I worked on creating a site where people could sell their digital products—music, ebooks, whatever. They would get a cut, and I would get a cut. I tried to make this thing fly with zero capital, but it never reached the end of the runway. I made $3.

I tried doing websites for people. I made a few bucks, but nothing impressive.

Miracles without money

Somewhere along the line my wife and I learned how to do transformational prayer. Amazing stuff. We prayed with people and saw incredible transformation. For example, I prayed with a woman who was torn up inside about having two abortions. God gave her a 45-minute vision in which she met her children in heaven. She got to hold them, talk to them, and they told her that they forgave her. It was astounding. (In some ways, I hesitate to tell you this because I NEVER recommend that you try to make contact with the dead, and there's no guarantee that someone else with identical circumstances would experience the same thing. But, even so, it was amazing.)

Wow! We've found our calling! We'll teach people how to do this! So we tried. My wife met with dozens of people to do this type of prayer. I wrote a textbook, created an online course, taught people how to do it.

Result? Never more than about $1,000 to $2,000 a year.

Somewhere in here I tried to start a church. For years I've been studying the church—what works, what doesn't, why people are leaving church. I felt like I had a prescription to fix all of that. I tried to assemble a team, but I didn't get what I needed. It was like trying to play baseball with only a pitcher and a catcher. It just didn't work.

Author Dwight Clough

I wrote several books. Some were published via traditional publishers. Most were self published. I always had high hopes for each book, but they never generated much income. Like usually less than $100 a year.

I worked on a new translation of the Bible. Again, I put together a team and negotiated an agreement with the person who held the trademark for the name I wanted to use. Despite my best efforts, I made less than ten cents per hour. Actually, I think I lost money.

Here's one scheme that did work, sort of: I started writing books for people. Yep, a ghostwriter. I figured if I could write full time, I could make 50-60K a year. But, it never seemed to turn out that way. Part of the problem is I got desperate. I took on projects I should have turned down. I wrote two or three books for the promise of money and hardly got paid anything. (I wrote a book on integrity for a client. He promised me $10,000 and never paid me a cent. Sometimes you just gotta laugh.)

Anyway, with ghostwriting, my income hovered around $15,000 a year. About the same as the sum of my mortgage payments.

$1 million offer with no money

Speaking of mortgage, we had our house. It was nearly 100 years old when we bought it. It seemed like every week something else broke down in it. I didn't have the money or the expertise to fix any of these things that went wrong.

So I got this idea. What if we tore down the house, and built an apartment building in its place? We could rent out the other apartments; the tenants could pay the mortgage, and we would live in a better house for free.

Just one problem. I didn't have any money to do it.

I was talking this over with a friend, and he said to me, "Dwight, you don't need money.

80

You have an idea. Other people have money. Just do it."

So I prayed about it and felt that God wanted me to stop dreaming and start doing. So I contacted an architect. I was desperately afraid he would charge me for having lunch with him because I had zero money to pay for even an hour of his time, but I met with him anyway.

To my surprise, he liked my idea. But, he said, the only way to make it work was to buy several of the adjoining properties, and build a bigger apartment building. Then I could get investors to help. My home happened to be in a TIF (tax increment financing) district, so the city would probably put some money into it as well.

Okay. A real estate friend helped me write options to purchase on two adjoining properties, and I spent weeks trying to negotiate with two other property owners to get a reasonable deal on their properties.

Meanwhile, we found a builder who wanted to work with us. Our architect drew up a concept—let me tell you it was beautiful. We kept meeting with the city, and they said, yes, yes, yes! And then…

No. No, we changed out mind. We don't like your idea.

However, they said, you can buy the 4 ½ acre site just down the street—the site of the former store, and convert that.

Remember, I have zero money. No money at all. And I'm being very up front with everybody about not having any money. But nobody seemed to care. It was okay. Like my friend said, I had the idea.

The owner of the 4 ½ acre site wanted $1.5 million for the property. We found a commercial real estate agent as well as a real estate attorney, and I offered him $750,000. A friend loaned me $15,000 at 10% so I could pay the earnest money and the attorney fees. We haggled with the owner for several months, and finally settled on a price of just over $1 million.

Which was interesting because my entire wealth consisted of questionable equity in a home that was falling apart. And since there was no way I could refinance my home with my income being at $15,000, there was no way to pull the money out of the home.

About this time I wrote a letter to Donald Trump asking him if he would mentor me and show me how to do this. I told him he could make it into a TV show. (This was before he ran for president.) No response, but, hey, it was a thought.

Donald Trump not available, I looked elsewhere and found partners. Rich guys. We formed an LLC, and my wife and I became 1/5 owners. Almost. We also had to put a big chunk of money into it, and since we didn't have that chunk of money, we ended up owing the LLC that amount plus interest.

For the next couple years, I attended regular meetings with our partners as we worked on how to redevelop this property. We had a vision to transform the property into an upscale mixed use (commercial and residential) development with 15,000 square feet of commercial space, 130 apartments with underground parking and some really cool amenities. To do that, we met with the city, with the architect, with prospective commercial tenants, with property managers, and the list goes on.

It was strange. One Thursday morning I put on a suit to meet with high powered attorneys downtown and discuss how we were going to get additional investors and lenders to put $30 million into this property. That Thursday evening I put on blue jeans to go to a food pantry to get groceries so our family wouldn't starve.

The only way this project made sense with the business model we had was for the city to put up a large amount of cash up front. $1 million plus. After many friendly meetings stretching over several months, it finally became clear that the city just wasn't going to do that. Meanwhile, the commercial tenant who was renting from us (and paying our expenses) left, and we couldn't find another tenant to take his place. We were hemorrhaging thousands of dollars every month.

About that time a different real estate developer came along and offered to buy the property from us. He offered just enough. We could all get out with money in our pockets.

No, I didn't make millions, but I walked away with a check in my hand—enough to help buy us another home.

Finding a home

About this time, my wife came up with a great idea: sell our home and rent it back from the new owner. (By this time our kids had all graduated from high school.) That way, we could pull our equity out of our home, have some cash, and maybe—just maybe, be able to pay cash to build a really, really cheap home somewhere out in the country.

We sold our home. Now, between cashing out of the LLC and selling our home, we had about $85,000 in cash—enough to pay off our credit card debt and still have a chunk of money left over.

We started with the crazy idea of buying some land cheap, parking an old RV on it, living in that until we could build a house with our own two hands from scratch without incurring any debt. We looked at log end home construction and figured we could learn how to do that if we could talk the building inspector into allowing us to use this form of alternative construction.

We made an offer on some land, and almost bought it, until we figured out (at the expense of several hundred dollars in attorney fees) that our neighbors would never give us an easement to get power to the site. And, to be honest, it looked like our one neighbor would probably like to use us for target practice. On top of that, the county really frowned on our living in an RV idea. That was a no go. So much for having a right to camp out on your own land.

What to do?

Very hesitantly, I met with the mortgage lender from our credit union.

"You actually have good credit," he said.

That was a shock.

"We could loan you up to …" Hmm. So we started looking for a house—something cheap enough we could actually afford.

We found one I really wanted to buy, but my wife vetoed that idea—thank God—because it flooded a few months later and was totally ruined.

We ended up finding a modest home on 1.6 acres of land out in the country. We made an offer, and now we live in it.

So that worked out nicely.

Scrambling

But, meanwhile, my ghostwriting business went down the drain. I felt like God wanted me to start teaching what I know about faith online, but try as I might to monetize that somehow, I ended up with zero. We kept losing money, watching our savings dwindle away.

I tried taking what I know about faith and transformation and creating online resources for sale. Total sales: Under $200.

My wife started an eBay business. After months of part-time effort, it started making a profit, but nowhere near minimum wage.

I tried selling used books online. First year: $30,000 in sales. Great, huh? Not really. $2,000 in profit.

Now I'm in my sixties. Even so, I haven't stopped dreaming. Here's one of my dreams: I want to make a movie. I want to explore the other side of "happily ever after" by making a movie of a man whose wife is dying of cancer. Before she dies, he just wants to know the answer to one question: *Was I your knight in shining armor?*

I don't know anything about making movies, but I'm just throwing it out there. Maybe the right kind of help will come back to me.

And, as you'll find out later, I'm working on a documentary.

Living by faith

Throughout my life I've lived by faith. I think that's one reason why I don't think of myself as poor. God always provides, often in creative ways. Let me give you an example:

The sump pump went out in our basement. To buy a new one meant I couldn't pay our bills that were due. So I didn't really want to buy another one, but our home couldn't function without it. I asked God to fix the pump for me, but I felt like He said, "No, I want you to buy one."

"Okay, I said, but please let me find a sump pump for under $100." (In my mind I'm thinking about how I'm going to shuffle bills around and probably end up paying something late.) Anyway, I got to the hardware store, and there on the shelf I found a sump pump for $99.99.

I took it up to the counter and it rang up for $119.00. I told the cashier that it was marked at $99.99.

"Oh, yeah," he said. "We made a mistake and put the wrong price on it. Thanks for catching that for us. We'll give you this one for $99.99."

I came home, installed the new sump pump, made sure it worked, and walked upstairs. Then I checked the mail. There in the mail was a totally unexpected check for $111.00.

This sort of thing happens to us a lot. One time my wife wanted a water distiller. The model she wanted was $400. We didn't have $400. So she asked God to provide it. She felt like God said to her, "If I give you $400, will you use it to buy the water distiller?" Kim said yes.

A couple weeks later, an old friend dropped by—someone we hadn't seen in a dozen years or longer. During her visit she said, "I just feel moved to give you this money." She handed us an envelope. Inside in cash was exactly $400.

Many times I've come to the last day of the month and had zero money to pay the rent or the mortgage. Yet somehow, on the first, the money came in. I got a new client or an unexpected rebate or an insurance settlement or a gift or who knows what. But somehow it always worked out. As a result of these experiences, I slowly learned to stop worrying about money—even when things looked hopeless.

For years, we never had money to buy clothes. Once, we were desperate to get shoes for our daughter, so we took money we really didn't have and bought her a pair. The next day, without knowing what we had done, someone went out and bought the exact same pair of shoes, and gave them to us.

Even though we didn't have money to buy clothes, we were never in want. We always had enough to wear. In fact, one year, we gave away 75 large trash bags filled with clothing. Somehow, God just provided.

Snapshots of life below the line

Having said that, I want to share some snapshots with you of what it was like for me living the life I've lived.

One of the reasons we've survived is this: I'm married to a world class money manager. During one stretch when we were doing okay financially—approaching the bottom end of middle class—I was able to give my wife some cash each week for groceries and household expenses. After a while, I asked her how things were going. She went to the closet, pulled out an envelope, and laid $800 out on the bed.

Wow.

I never wanted to take charity from anyone. I think a lot of people assume that the poor are just leeches who would rather sponge than work. I've never felt that way.

We went without medical insurance because we couldn't afford it. Then our daughter was born with a club foot. She needed two surgeries, and the medical bills were piling up much, much faster than our ability to pay. So we turned to Medicaid to pay the bill, and kept it so that all of our children could have medical care. It really came in handy when one of our kids was in the ICU for five days. I never saw the bill, but I wouldn't be surprised if it was north of $100,000.

I never wanted food stamps. But we were down to one meal a day as a family. We were scrounging through the house looking for loose change so we could buy something to eat. I remember standing in a store looking at a can of beans that sold for 65 cents. I was so hungry, and that can of beans looked so good, but I didn't have 65 cents. Soon after that, I applied for food stamps.

Years later, when my kids were in high school and started to earn money with their own part time employment, the food stamp benefit evaporated. I understand their reasoning. Put together the incomes of the parents and the four teens, and you don't need food stamps any more. But I wasn't about to tell my kids that they needed to surrender their paychecks to me so I could buy groceries for them. I wanted them to be able to save up their money so they could go to college or do some of the things they really wanted to do. So we had the same food needs without the assistance. That's why I started getting groceries at a food pantry.

Even so, I'm glad I let my kids keep most of their money. (I did charge them a modest sum for room and board after they graduated from high school.) As a result—and largely due to money they earned on their own—my kids have been able to travel to Australia, Nepal, China, Japan, Papua New Guinea—to do medical missionary outreach, to do compassion missions, for educational purposes, or just to experience a different slice of life. This is something I always wanted to do, but was never able to do, so I'm glad they have had the opportunity. And they earned it themselves, working at McDonald's, at Wal-Mart, or the like.

I've learned over the years to keep quiet about our financial needs. I've served on teams in churches where we've tried to look for opportunities to help the poor. That was a surreal experience. Here I was—probably the poorest person they knew, and yet we were discussing how we would help the poor "out there" by volunteering or giving money to a food pantry or a homeless shelter.

And if I said something about our financial struggles, the response was almost always the same: I'm middle class. Why aren't you middle class? If you're not middle class, there must be something wrong with you. You must be, in some way, morally deficient. Lazy. Yep, you're probably lazy. You're lazy, and you deserve to be poor. And, by the way, don't talk to me about your poverty. It makes me feel uncomfortable. I'm middle class. And I don't want to feel uncomfortable.

Of course, they didn't use those words. They were more polite. But, hey, I can deconstruct what someone is actually saying just as well as the next guy.

At times I've brought up our financial struggles with some members of our extended family. The response has mostly been disgusted silence. Again, I can read between the lines. I know what people are thinking.

So, no, I don't talk about being poor. And people usually don't talk to me about it. Maybe I act middle class. Maybe I blend in. I don't know.

On the other hand, many people have been extraordinarily kind and generous to us over the years. When we were homeless, someone let us stay in her basement part of the week, and others let us stay with them at other times. People have bought groceries for us— one person came over to our home, and, unknown to us, carefully studied what food we had, and went out and bought the same brands that we liked.

Other people have been generous with their time and their advice, helping us make better business, marketing, and financial decisions. Several people have sacrificed a great deal of time to provide what guidance they could to help us do better. I am humbled and grateful for the kindness shown by these good people.

Gratitude and hope

I want you to know that I'm not complaining. I love my life. I'm deeply grateful for my life. But I do want to do better financially. I'm 62 years old, and I have major expenses looming ahead: retirement, long term care, weddings for my daughters, college and medical care for my four kids, long term care for my mom, and more. And our adjusted gross income last year was…well, let's just say it wasn't that high.

Over the years, a number of people have offered advice and counsel. I'm deeply grateful for that. I've tried my best to learn from each person, and put into practice the lessons that seem to apply to me. I remain filled with hope that something will come together—something will work for my family and for me.

Takeaway

I've sat in welfare offices. I can tell you that there are few places in this world that are gloomier. The very architecture exudes contempt for the clients these offices serve. The signage, the locked barrier between the waiting room and the offices—it all speaks of class division, class contempt. There's no sense of partnership, no sense of teamwork, no sense of working together. While I've had many conversations with caseworkers, not once has anyone said, "Tell me about yourself. Talk to me about your strengths and weaknesses, your interests and abilities. Let's see if we can figure out the best pathway out of poverty for you." Instead, the conversations were always centered around making sure that I wasn't committing welfare fraud. Since I was self employed, I didn't have pay stubs. So I needed to produce profit and loss statements, or, later years, income tax records. That's all. That's the only help I got.

In my mind, that's tragic. If I had had a mentor, someone who took the time to understand what I'm all about, what I offer my world, and helped me figure out how and where to best monetize that, then I would have saved the taxpayer multiplied tens of thousands of dollars in Medicaid and food stamps. But that never happened. I tried my best to figure it out on my own, and I'm still trying.

My situation is, admittedly, unique. But then everyone's situation is unique. Every person deserves to be treated as an individual. Every person is a bundle of untapped potential. With the right encouragement, the right training, the right mentoring, all kinds of real wealth could be released for the benefit of everyone.

If I could push rewind, I would have forged through and obtained my PhD. Without it, I feel like I'm functioning way below my potential. Likewise, I wish we could make education more accessible to all Americans. I understand the concerns conservatives have over taxpayers paying the bill for everyone to get a free ride to college. And I have my own set of concerns: As soon as the government starts paying for something, the government hungers to control it, to micromanage it, to make it an ideological weapon in the hands of polarized politicians. That's their goal with K-12 public schools, and that would be their goal with higher education as well. If we could some-how get beyond that, then giving each person access to the education or training that's right for them would unleash all kinds of potential.

Everybody needs a mentor. Everybody needs a coach. I needed one, but didn't have one. I hope things can be different for future generations.

Footnote: About me

If you're interested in learning any more about me, reading the books I've written, or exploring the what I offer, you can find me at DwightClough.com …

A prayer for our country

God,

if You please …

Let truth triumph over deception.

Let justice and mercy triumph over injustice.

Let understanding, respect, trust, and love triumph over polarization.

Amen.

Conclusion: How to win the war

I drew some pictures for you:

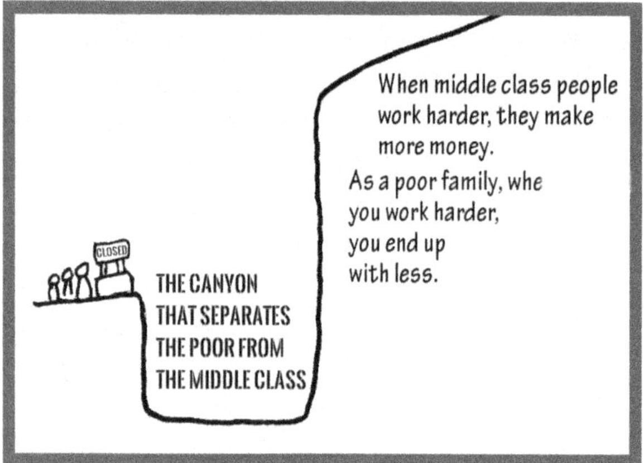

To move from poverty to middle class, multiple canyons must be crossed, and those canyons are different for different people.

Sometimes those canyons are inside the minds of the individual person living below the line. For a long time, I couldn't think straight because I was so stressed, living in survival mode. I hardly slept at night, and during the day my mind was so crowded with stress that there was no room to think clearly about solutions. Other people, especially those who live in generational poverty, may be telling themselves stories that aren't true: *This is normal. This is your life; there's nothing you can do about it.* And so on. Or they may have unconsciously adopted patterns of behavior that block their way forward.

Sometimes the canyons come from the culture in which poor people live. For example, many people living below the line must fight against the "crab bucket" mentality that pulls people back down when they try to climb out.

Sometimes the canyons come from exploitation—whether intentional or not—people and systems take advantage of the vulnerability of the poor just because they can.

And sometimes the canyons come from the very systems that are supposed to help the poor. Often people designing these systems imagine the world with a "middle class mind," not taking into account the chaos that is an every day part of living in poverty.'

In fact, our war against poverty has created some of the biggest barriers to leaving poverty. How do we normally fight poverty? With benefits. You're hungry? Okay, we'll give you food—food stamps, food pantries. You need medical care? Okay, we'll give you Medicaid. You need child care so you can work? Okay, free child care. Money for college? Pell grants. Low income? Earned Income Credit (EIC). And so on.

So what happens when the poor make incremental improvements in their income? These benefits start dropping away. That's why the poor in low paying jobs sometimes don't want a raise. They can't afford it. That extra $100 a month causes them to lose their free child care, lose their food stamps, lose their health insurance, and so on. Do the math. They don't have that kind of money. It's expensive to be poor.

In short, our war against poverty traps people inside poverty. When middle class people work harder, they end up with more. When poor people work harder, they end up with less.

Why don't we win the war on poverty? The answer is simple. We don't help people get out of poverty.

That's it. It really is not any more complicated than that.

Let's talk about that.

First of all, while this is improving, why do so many still think that helping one another is a bad thing? That mindset is a disease in our culture. Sure, a certain amount of competitiveness and rugged individualism is fine—it makes us the country that we are. But this notion that we need to win by making other people lose is sick. And it's not true. Your success does not diminish me. It enriches me. When you hurt, I hurt. And, besides, I'm sorry, but nobody got to "the top" alone. Anybody who climbed the ladder of success had help. Let's have the humility to acknowledge that, and then let's reach out and help one another.

So, yes, the poor need help, but they need the right kind of help. If someone comes along to help you who doesn't respect you, doesn't listen to you, thinks he's better than you, tries to push you into doing things that aren't you, how receptive are you going to be?

Exactly.

So any help must depart from the smarter-than-thou social engineering of some. It must be built on a foundation of respect and understanding. It must acknowledge that each person is an individual with his or her own set of strengths, weaknesses, opportunities, and threats. There are no cookie cutter solutions. The poor are not cattle to be herded.

Crafting an individual route out of poverty takes time. It isn't accomplished in a 15 minute meeting where you say, "You need to get a job." Sorry, middle class thinker. Rewind. Stop. Listen.

What does it take to get someone out of poverty? A lot.

If you give me a random person living in poverty, will I know how to get that person out?

Probably not.

You probably won't either.

But _we_ will. By we, I mean the collective intelligence of 328 million Americans. Some-one(s) will know how to get that person out of poverty. There are people out there who can figure this out. _We_ can solve poverty for that person if we want to.

Do we want to?

#4 They invest whatever it takes
to empower you to get out
of poverty forever

#5 They advocate for you
and don't leave you stranded
in the canyon that separates
the poor from the middle class.
Instead, they give you tools
to cross that canyon.

Okay, I've had people sit down with me and spend an hour trying to help me figure out how to get out of poverty. Did I appreciate their efforts? Depends. Sometimes they were so out of touch with who I am and the world I live in that I just had to endure the meeting. But more often they were good people who truly listened and took into account where I was coming from. In those cases, yes, I was profoundly grateful for their help. I listened, and I tried to apply their suggestions. But I didn't escape poverty's gravitational pull.

My point?

Helping the poor get out of poverty isn't easy. It takes time. It isn't a sprint. It's a marathon.

I spoke with a friend who met with a single mom weekly for a year. He was frustrated because she wasn't following all of his suggestions.

Welcome to reality! If it was easy to get the poor out of poverty, they would have already done it themselves.

We need mentors who are gonna help us cross these canyons—whether the canyons are systems, people, or inner barriers created by our own minds.

That means mentors will need to invest time, money, creativity, empathy, expertise, and whatever else is needed. Mentors cannot be defeated by setbacks because setbacks are part of the journey to success. We need mentors who are prepared to stay with us until we cross the finish line.

But when we do cross that line, great things happen.

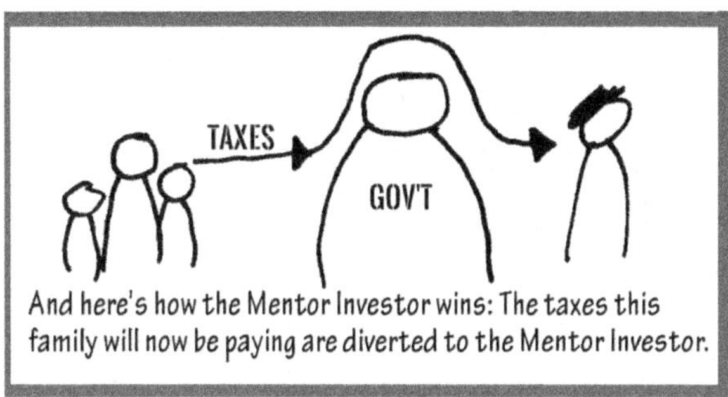

And here's how the Mentor Investor wins: The taxes this family will now be paying are diverted to the Mentor Investor.

My son Hans has a simple solution to the criminal justice quagmire. Here it is: Privatize all the prisons. Then fund them according to how long their "graduates" stay out of trouble.

I like that. Sure, it might need tweaking, but at its heart it employs something the government has forgotten to do:

Fund success.

Right now, when it comes to the war on poverty, we fund failure. We pay people to stay in poverty, we don't pay them to get out. We penalize them for even trying to get out of poverty. On top of that, we pay welfare workers to keep people in poverty. It's definitely NOT to their economic advantage to get people out of poverty. If they get enough people out of poverty, they lose their jobs. What a messed up system!

Ending poverty is very simple. Fund success.

Pay for results. When you pay for results, somebody somewhere will find a way to deliver those results.

And what's so terrible about rewarding people who help other people?

How does the Mentor Investor™ get paid? The family s/he helped is no longer poor. That family is now paying taxes. The government diverts those tax payments back to the Mentor Investor™.

I call this Tax Diversion Financing™. It's a simple way to reward the Mentor Investor™ for his/her/their efforts.

Getting people out of poverty is a huge job. Those who do it successfully should be rewarded. And I don't care how rich or poor they were before they started helping someone else; they should be rewarded regardless.

And here's the magic of this. Rewarding Mentor Investors™ doesn't really cost the government a dime. On the contrary, the government realizes a net gain because it no longer needs to pay benefits. That is a huge savings.

And we already do something like this with TIF financing (tax increment financing). When local governments want to entice developers into redeveloping a blighted area, they offer to suspend or rebate property tax payments for several years in order to help finance the development. This is a similar idea. We're just rewarding the people who make the huge investment needed to get someone out of poverty.

I believe there is a path out of poverty for every person—every family below the poverty line. That path will look a little different for each person. For some people, all they need is a job—the right job. But for most, the need is more complex than that. New skills need to be learned. Inner barriers need to be broken.

In every case, individuals should be listened to, understood, respected, and honored for who they are and for the real value they offer their families, their communities, their nation, and their world.

The Mentor Investors™ who make this happen are going to make friends with some beautiful people who are presently locked in the prison of poverty. Setting them free will be an incredibly rewarding experience.

While many will cross over into the middle class, I believe some will transition from poverty to wealth. In some ways, I think the poor are better candidates for wealth than the middle class as they don't have some of the same baggage about money and possessions that the middle class need to shed in order to transition into wealth.

In any case, this is a winnable war. This is an achievable goal.

You have a role

Here's what's next.

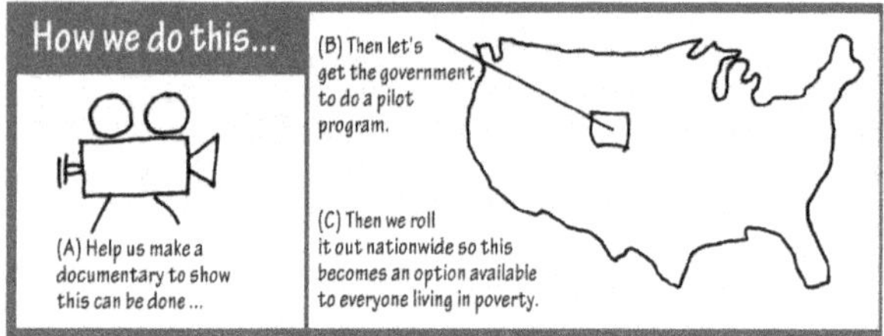

As I write this, we're working on a documentary. The goal of our film is to create a movement to help people get out of poverty.

Our film will feature stories and insights from "below the line" as well as stories from those who have crossed the line from poverty into middle class and beyond. We will include expert interviews. And I've already talked to one celebrity who has expressed an interest in appearing in the film. I hope you and I can attract several more. To help us tell our story, I've engaged the services of a filmmaker with extensive experience making poverty-related documentaries.

Here's how you can help.

The first step to solving poverty is seeing the poor through a different set of eyes. We need leaders to help our country begin to do that. If you and I can find celebrities of all types from across the political spectrum who will help us do that, this is a big win for the poor.

Who do you know? Do you know someone who knows someone? Can you get us connected?

Doing this right won't be cheap. We need people who can help us raise the money we need. To put this together, we'll need attorneys, air miles, advertising, consultants, phone calls, and a zillion other things as well. Please don't think that your contribution will be too small. It won't. We need you.

Can you get us connected? Email me at DwightClough@gmail.com with "Together documentary" in the subject line.

And check WeWillEndPoverty.com to see what our latest needs are.

After we finish the documentary, our next step will be to work with federal and state lawmakers to set up a pilot program to test our Tax Diversion Financing™ concept.

And, yes, of course, there will be bugs. Of course, there will be fraud. You can't move forward without encountering those kinds of things. That's why we do a pilot program—to get the bugs out of it before we roll it out nationwide.

This can be done. The war on poverty can be won.

But it really starts with you, right here, right now.

Who needs a copy of this book? Who do you know who needs to join our movement?

The next five minutes belong to you. What are you going to do with them?

It's your move…

www.ingramcontent.com/pod-product-compliance
Lightning Source LLC
Chambersburg PA
CBHW070733250726

48662CB00004B/1523

9798636098041